About the Author

I0016693

Paul Watson is a technology enthusiast an
experience in various technologies like we.   ....
development, automation testing, build automation,
continuous integration and deployment technologies. He
has worked on most of the technology stacks.
He has hands on experience on UFT, LeanFT, Selenium and
Appium. He has used testing frameworks like JUnit,
TestNG, Cucumber with Selenium. He has also worked on
Struts, Spring, Bootstratp, Angular JS.

His hobbies include travelling to new tourist places,
watching basketball, cricket and learning latest
technological stuff.

A special note of Thanks to My Wife

I would like to dedicate this book to my lovely wife for loving me so much and helping me write this book. Without her support, this book would not have been a reality.

Who this book is for

This book is for automation engineers who want to learn LeanFT to automate the web and windows applications in C#.Net.

It is assumed that reader has a basic programming skills in C#.Net language. Whether you are a beginner or an experienced developer, this book will help you master the skills on LeanFT.

The book starts with introduction of LeanFT and then dives into key concepts as mentioned below.

Installation of LeanFT, Installing the browser extensions, Setting up LeanFT project in Visual Studio, LeanFT Settings, Object identification center, Understanding LeanFT API in C#.Net, Understanding LeanFT API in C#.Net, Object identification center, Automating windows application, Running first test, Integrating LeanFT with Visual Studio Unit testing framework, Viewing the results of the test, Description programming in LeanFT, Creating the application models, Using regular expressions in LeanFT, Web application testing using LeanFT, Identifying the elements using xpath and css, Firing events, Executing JavaScript, Calculator automation using LeanFT, Notepad Automation using LeanFT, Automation of Java Applications, Automation of SAP Applications, Automation of .Net Applications, Using Visual Relational Identifier, Synchronization ,Assertions and reports ,Converting UFT object repository into application model ,Frameworks in LeanFT, Integrating the LeanFT tests with CI servers like

LeanFT in C#.Net

Bamboo (MSBuild and MSTest), Jenkins and TeamCity, Challenges and solutions , Comparison of LeanFT with Selenium and Ranorex, Difference between HP UFT and LeanFT.

Table of Contents

1. LeanFT Basics

1.1 LeanFT Introduction

LeanFT stands for Lean Functional testing. This is a tool developed by HP and very similar to the Ranorex.

Key points to note about LeanFT are given below.

1. It's a licensed tool.
2. Developed by HP in 2015.
3. It's light version of UFT (QTP).
4. With LeanFT, you can write tests in .Net language as well as Java.
5. LeanFT plugin are available for Visual Studio and Eclipse.
6. LeanFT uses description programming as well as Application models to identify the objects.

1.2 Supported applications by LeanFT

LeanFT supports below types of applications.

1. Web applications on IE, Chrome, Firefox, Microsoft Edge
2. Windows application - WPF, Silverlight and more
3. SAP applications
4. Java applications
5. Standard windows and forms

In fact, all applications supported by UFT (QTP) are also supported by LeanFT.

2. Installation of LeanFT

2.2 Installation of LeanFT

First visit https://saas.hpe.com/en-us/software/leanft and download the trail version of LeanFT.

Before starting the installation process of LeanFT, ensure below things

1. You have a node.js and IDE tools (Visual Studio, IntelliJ IDEA, Eclipse) already installed on your system.
2. Anti-virus software is disabled

At the time of installation, you will choose which plugins to be installed.
By default, LeanFT is installed at C:\Program Files (x86)\HP\LeanFT
Once installed, start the LeanFT engine (from installation directory or from Start menu of Windows). By default, LeanFT service runs on port 5095

Below screen shot shows the installation options during installation process. Please select full installation with visual studio and Eclipse options checked.

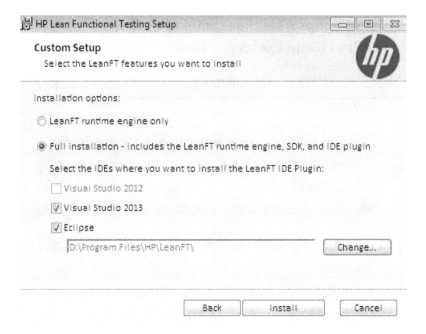

If you have got IntelliJ installed on your system, you will see below screen. Just select the checkbox next to IntelliJ IDEA to install the LeanFT plugin for IntelliJ IDEA.

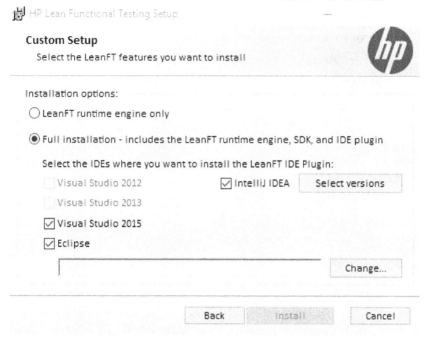

LeanFT plugins

After installation of LeanFT, start the runtime engine as shown in below image. By default, engine runs on the port 5095.

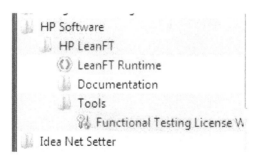

2.2 Installing the browser extensions

After installation of LeanFT, you can view the browser extension files at below location in LeanFT installation directory.

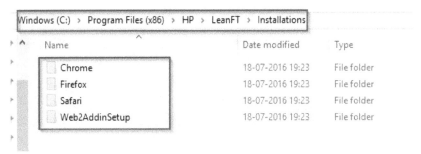

Browser extensions for LeanFT

Just drag and drop the extension files on the browsers. Browser will install these extensions when you drop these extension files on it.

Without installing and enabling these extensions in browsers, you will not be able to automate the web application.

Below image shows the LeanFT extension enabled in chrome browser.

Extensions

☐ Developer

Google Slides   0.9

☑ Enabled

Create and edit presentations

Details

☐ Allow in incognito

HP Functional Testing Agent   12.53.2027.0

☑ Enabled

Test Web Applications Using Google Chrome

Details   Options

☐ Allow in incognito   ☐ Allow access to file URLs

LeanFT extension in Chrome

3. Setting up LeanFT project in Visual Studio

Setting up the LeanFT project in Visual Studio is very simple.

We can set up the LeanFT project in Visual Studio in 2 ways.

1. Using LeanFT test templates
2. Your own custom C# Project

Below screen shot shows the new project window in Visual Studio. When you select the test template category, you will see below LeanFT templates. You can use MsTest Project.

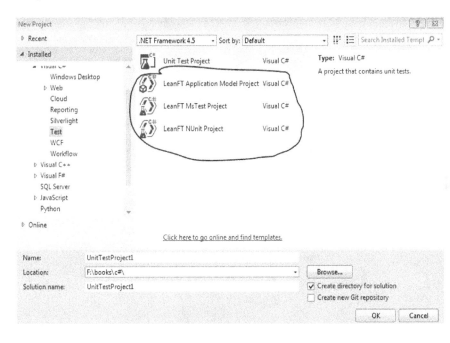

To create your own LeanFT project, you can just select the Unit testing project.

Once you create a new project, you will have to add the LeanFT reference libraries in your project. Reference libraries are located in the LeanFT installation folder as shown in below image.

Name	Date modified	Type
Dependencies	12-09-2015 12:52	File folder
HP.LFT.Common.dll	02-07-2015 09:41	DLL File
HP.LFT.Report.dll	02-07-2015 09:41	DLL File
HP.LFT.SDK.dll	02-07-2015 09:41	DLL File
HP.LFT.SDK.XML	02-07-2015 09:19	XML Document
HP.LFT.UnitTesting.dll	02-07-2015 09:41	DLL File

4. LeanFT settings

4.1 LeanFT Settings

You can open LeanFT engine and object identification settings from LeanFT Plugin menu option as shown in below image.

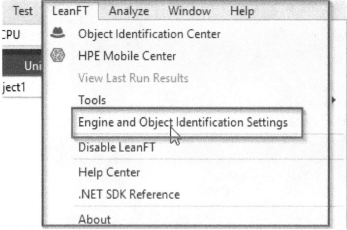

Engine and Object Identification Settings in LeanFT

Below image shows how to configure plug-ins in LeanFT.

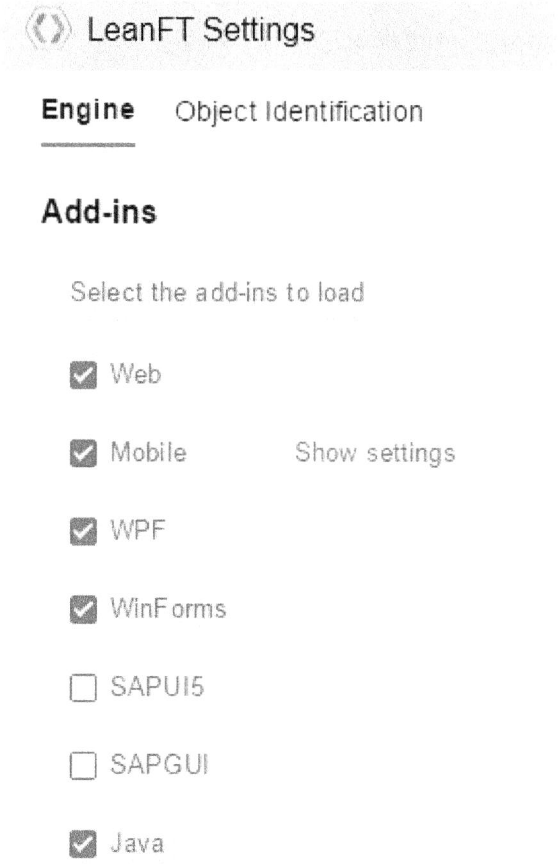

⟨⟩ LeanFT Settings

Engine   Object Identification

Add-ins

Select the add-ins to load

☑ Web

☑ Mobile   Show settings

☑ WPF

☑ WinForms

☐ SAPUI5

☐ SAPGUI

☑ Java

Below image shows that we can configure the LeanFT port and Engine idle timeout. It also shows setting for object synchronization timeout.

Engine Connection

Port	Engine idle timeout (in minutes)
5095	240

Runtime settings

Object synchronization timeout (in seconds)
20

☐ Allow LeanFT to run tests on a disconnected RDP computer

User name	Password
	••••••••••••••••••••••

Engine connection and object synchronization timeout in LeanFT

Below image shows which properties are used by LeanFT to identify the objects.

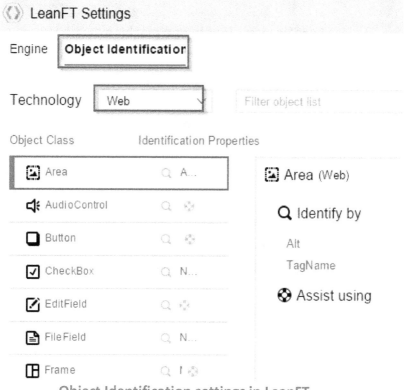

Object Identification settings in LeanFT

4.2 Types of Licenses in LeanFT

LeanFT comes with 4 types of licenses as shown in below image.

1. Seat License - Tied to one machine
2. Concurrent license - Multiple machines can use this license
3. Commuter license
4. Remote commuter license

Functional Testing License Wizard 🛈

SELECT LICENSE TYPE

 Seat license
Install a personal license for this machine

🗸 Active License
Until 13-10-2015

 Concurrent license
Install a session-based license from the license server

 Commuter license
Obtain/install commuter licenses for this machine

 Remote commuter license
Request and install commuter licenses for this machine when you do not have access to the license server

5. Core Concepts

5.1 Object identification center

You can launch Object Identification Center in visual studio by clicking on the object identification center menu item under LeanFT menu.

Below screenshot shows the Object Identification Center showing the properties of the Calculator window.

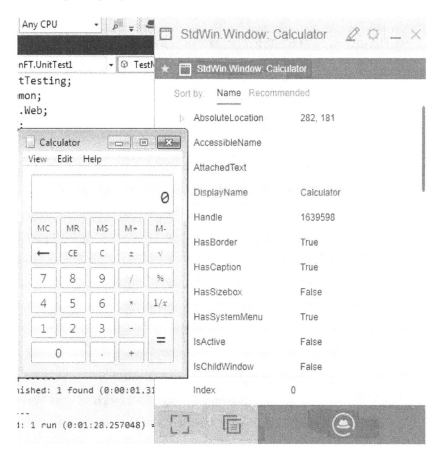

The rectangle tool in the bottom is used to highlight the object. Another important tool is code generator (Just adjacent to the highlight tool).

When I hit the generate code button, below code was generated to identify the calculator window.

```
Desktop.Describe<IWindow>(new
WindowDescription
{
IsOwnedWindow = false,
IsChildWindow = false,
WindowClassRegExp = @"CalcFrame",
WindowTitleRegExp = @"Calculator"
});
```

5.2 Understanding LeanFT API in C#.Net

Here are the namespaces in LeanFT API in C#.Net

1. HP.LFT.REPORT - contains the Reporter and ReportConfiguration classes used to configure the reports.
2. HP.LFT.SDK - contains namespaces for various technologies like WPF, Web, Standard Windows, SAP, Java etc.
3. HP.LFT.UnitTesting - provides the classes required for LeanFT testing framework
4. HP.LFT.Verifications - contains Verify class that can be used to do assertions in LeanFT tests.

6. Understanding LeanFT plugin in Visual Studio

LeanFT plugin is installed in Visual studio automatically when you install the LeanFT runtime engine (Full installation).

When you launch visual studio, you will see LeanFT plugin as shown in below image.

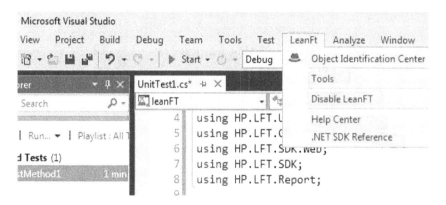

LeanFT plugin provides below items.

1. Object identification center (Just like object spy)
2. Tools (Password encoder)
3. Help center (General help on LeanFT)
4. .Net SDK reference (Documentation on LeanFT library)

7. Understanding LeanFT API in C#.Net
Here are the namespaces in LeanFT API in C#.Net

1. HP.LFT.REPORT - contains the Reporter and ReportConfiguration classes used to configure the reports.
2. HP.LFT.SDK - contains namespaces for various technologies like WPF, Web, Standard Windows, SAP, Java etc.
3. HP.LFT.UnitTesting - provides the classes required for LeanFT testing framework
4. HP.LFT.Verifications - contains Verify class that can be used to do assertions in LeanFT tests.

8. First LeanFT test in Visual Studio

8.1 Automating windows application

Now we are going to write one test to verify the calculator functionality using LeanFT.

We want to do below things.

1. Launch calculator application.
2. Check the title of the calculator window.
3. Click 8 button and Verify the result.
4. Close the calculator.

Below program will perform all above operations. Please note that I have used Object Identification Center to get the description code for the calculator objects. Note that below code will work only on windows 7 calculator. The calculator app in windows 10 is designed using different technology.

```
using System;
using
Microsoft.VisualStudio.TestTools.UnitTesting;
using HP.LFT.SDK.Descriptions;
using HP.LFT.UnitTesting;
using HP.LFT.Common;
using HP.LFT.SDK.Web;
using HP.LFT.SDK;
using HP.LFT.Report;
using HP.LFT.SDK.StdWin;
using System.Diagnostics;

namespace leanFT
{
    [TestClass]
```

```
    public class UnitTest1
    {

        [TestMethod]
        public void TestCalculator()
        {
            SDK.Init(new SdkConfiguration());
            Reporter.Init(new
ReportConfiguration());

Process.Start(@"d:\Windows\System32\calc.exe");
            IWindow win =
Desktop.Describe<IWindow>(new WindowDescription
                {
                    IsOwnedWindow = false,
                    IsChildWindow = false,
                    WindowClassRegExp =
@"CalcFrame",
                    WindowTitleRegExp =
@"Calculator"
                });

            Trace.WriteLine("Calculator window
title is " + win.WindowTitleRegExp);


            var button8 =
win.Describe<HP.LFT.SDK.StdWin.IButton>(new
HP.LFT.SDK.StdWin.ButtonDescription
                {
                    Text = string.Empty,
                    WindowId = 138,
                    NativeClass = @"Button"
                });
            button8.Click();

            var result =
win.Describe<IStatic>(new StaticDescription
                {
                    WindowId = 150,
```

```
                NativeClass = @"Static"
            });
        Trace.WriteLine("Result text contains
" + result.Text);
            win.Close();
            Reporter.GenerateReport();
            SDK.Cleanup();
        }
    }
}
```

8.2 Running first test

Now that we have created the test, let us run it.

Visual studio comes with test explorer window which allows easy option to run the tests. All tests in our project are listed in the test explorer which we can run.

Below image shows the test explorer in visual studio 2013. In below test explorer, we have 2 tests - TestCalculator and TestMethod1. It's also showing the result for the TestCalculator test.

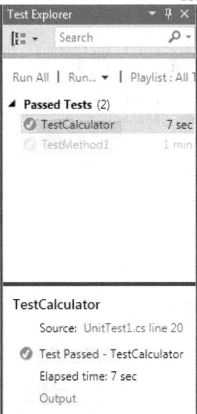

8.3 Integrating LeanFT with Visual Studio Unit testing framework

Here is the example that shows how to integrate LeanFT with Visual Studio Unit testing framework. Note that we have initialized the LeanFT SDK at the beginning of the code and cleaned it up at the end.

```csharp
using System;
using
Microsoft.VisualStudio.TestTools.UnitTesting;
using HP.LFT.SDK;
using HP.LFT.Report;
using System.Diagnostics;
using System.Threading;
using HP.LFT.SDK.StdWin;

namespace LeanFtTestProject1
{
    [TestClass]
    public class UnitTest1
    {
        [TestMethod]
        public void TestMethod1()
        {
            SDK.Init(new SdkConfiguration
            {
                ServerAddress = new
Uri("ws://localhost:5095")
            });
            Reporter.Init(new
ReportConfiguration());

            Process appProcess = new Process {
StartInfo = { FileName =
@"C:\Windows\System32\notepad.exe" } };
            appProcess.Start();

            Thread.Sleep(3000);

            IWindow notepadWindow =
Desktop.Describe<IWindow>(new WindowDescription
            {
                WindowClassRegExp = "Notepad",
                WindowTitleRegExp = " Notepad"
            });
```

```
        IEditor editor =
notepadWindow.Describe<IEditor>(new
EditorDescription
        {
            WindowClassRegExp = "Edit",
            NativeClass = "Edit"
        });

        editor.SendKeys("This is automated
text");

        Reporter.GenerateReport();
        SDK.Cleanup();
      }
    }
}
```

8.4 Viewing the results of the test

After LeanFT tests are executed, reports are generated
and put in the below directory of the project.

\bin\Debug\RunResults

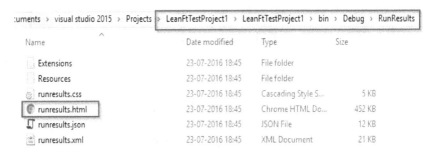

Viewing run results of LeanFT tests in Visual Studio

Below image shows sample HTML report for LeanFT tests.

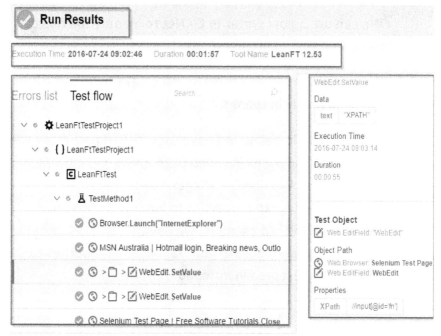

HTML report in LeanFT - Visual Studio

9. Object identification and Management

9.1 Description programming in LeanFT

We can use below syntax in C#.Net to identify the objects using Description programming.

We can pass multiple property-value pairs to identify the object uniquely in LeanFT.

In first example below, we have used XPATH property to identify the input box in a web page. In second example, we have used WindowClassRegExp and WindowTitleRegExp properties to identify the notepad Window. In the last example, we have used WindowClassRegExp and NativeClass properties to identify the text area in notepad.

```
// Find edit box using Xpath
            IEditField firstName =
browser.Describe <IEditField>(new
EditFieldDescription
            {
                XPath = "//input[@id='fn']"

            });

  IWindow notepadWindow =
Desktop.Describe<IWindow>(new WindowDescription
            {
                WindowClassRegExp = "Notepad",
                WindowTitleRegExp = " Notepad"
            });

   IEditor editor =
notepadWindow.Describe<IEditor>(new
EditorDescription
```

```
            {
                WindowClassRegExp = "Edit",
                NativeClass = "Edit"
            });
```

9.2 Creating the application models

There are 2 ways to create or manage the test objects in LeanFT.

1. Description programming
2. Application model (Just like old Object repository in UFT)

In this article, we are going to see how to create the application model from scratch and access it in the code.

In your visual studio project, you will have to add the new application model item as shown in below image.

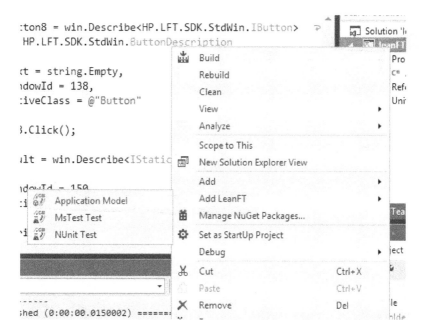

Below screen shot shows the new application model with one object (Calculator window) added into it.

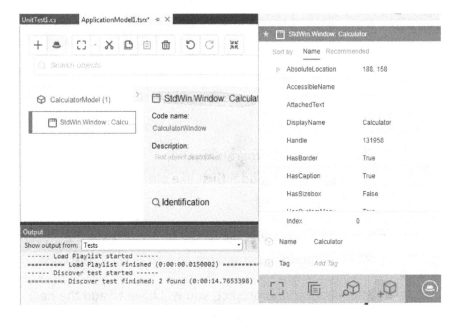

Once your model is ready, you can access it from the code as shown in below lines.

```
var calculatorModel = new CalculatorModel();
calculatorModel.CalculatorWindow.ButtonPlus.Cli
ck();
```

Here is the complete example on calculator addition operator. Please note that to use models, you need to add reference of System.Drawing namespace into your project

```
using System;
using
Microsoft.VisualStudio.TestTools.UnitTesting;
using HP.LFT.SDK.Descriptions;
using HP.LFT.UnitTesting;
using HP.LFT.Common;
```

```csharp
using HP.LFT.SDK.Web;
using HP.LFT.SDK;
using HP.LFT.Report;
using HP.LFT.SDK.StdWin;
using System.Diagnostics;

namespace leanFT
{
    [TestClass]
    public class UnitTest1
    {

        [TestMethod]
        public void TestCalculator()
        {
            SDK.Init(new SdkConfiguration());
            Reporter.Init(new
ReportConfiguration());

Process.Start(@"d:\Windows\System32\calc.exe");
            IWindow win =
Desktop.Describe<IWindow>(new WindowDescription
                {
                    IsOwnedWindow = false,
                    IsChildWindow = false,
                    WindowClassRegExp =
@"CalcFrame",
                    WindowTitleRegExp =
@"Calculator"
                });

            Trace.WriteLine("Calculator window
title is " + win.WindowTitleRegExp);

            var button8 =
win.Describe<HP.LFT.SDK.StdWin.IButton>(new
HP.LFT.SDK.StdWin.ButtonDescription
                {
                    Text = string.Empty,
                    WindowId = 138,
```

```
                    NativeClass = @"Button"
            });
            button8.Click();

            var result =
win.Describe<IStatic>(new StaticDescription
            {
                WindowId = 150,
                NativeClass = @"Static"
            });
            Trace.WriteLine("Result text contains
" + result.Text);

            var calculatorModel = new
CalculatorModel();

calculatorModel.CalculatorWindow.ButtonPlus.Cli
ck();

calculatorModel.CalculatorWindow.Button3.Click(
);

calculatorModel.CalculatorWindow.ButtonEquals.C
lick();
            Trace.WriteLine("Result of addition
is " + result.Text);
            Assert.AreEqual("11", result.Text,
"Addition of 8 and 3");
            win.Close();
            Reporter.GenerateReport();
            SDK.Cleanup();
        }
    }
}
```

9.3 Using regular expressions in LeanFT

Regular expressions are really useful to identify the objects in LeanFT.

We can specify the property values as regular expressions in 2 ways.

1. Using description programming
2. Using application model editor

Example with Description programming

Suppose you want to click on the link which contains text Softpost. In this scenario you can write the property value as shown in below statement.

```
var leanFTLink = browser.Describe<ILink>(new
LinkDescription
{
TagName = @"A",
InnerText =As.RegExp(@".*LeanFT.*"),
Index = 1
});
```

Example with Application model editor

In application model editor, we can specify the regular expression as shown in below image. You just need to click on the * icon in front of the property value which you want to make as a regular expression.

🔲 StdWin.Button: Button1

Code name:

Button3

Description:

Test object description

🔍 Identification   Used

Object properties

✅ NativeClass   (✱)Button

✅ Text   Set as regular expression

✅ WindowId   133

10. Web applications automation

10.1 Web application testing using LeanFT

In this article, we will see how to automate web application with different browsers like Internet explorer, Firefox and chrome.

Before you dive into the automation of browsers, ensure that HP Functional testing agent add-on (extension) is installed and enabled in your browsers.

Below code will launch softpost.org and then click on first link containing text as "LeanFT". We can use below example with little tweaks to handle many scenarios.

For example - Suppose on the given page, there is a list of links with transaction ids and you want to click on the first link. In this scenario, you can change the InnerText property of the link so that LeanFT will identify the link.

```
InnerText =As.RegExp(@"\d*")
```

```
using System;
using
Microsoft.VisualStudio.TestTools.UnitTesting;
using HP.LFT.SDK.Descriptions;
using HP.LFT.UnitTesting;
using HP.LFT.Common;
using HP.LFT.SDK.Web;
using HP.LFT.SDK;
using HP.LFT.Report;
using HP.LFT.SDK.StdWin;
using System.Diagnostics;

namespace leanFT
```

```csharp
{
    [TestClass]
    public class UnitTest1
    {
        [TestMethod]
        public void VerifySoftPost()
        {
            SDK.Init(new SdkConfiguration());
            Reporter.Init(new
ReportConfiguration());
            IBrowser browser =
BrowserFactory.Launch(BrowserType.InternetExplo
rer);

            browser.Navigate("softpost.org");

            var leanFTLink =
browser.Describe<ILink>(new LinkDescription
            {
                TagName = @"A",
                InnerText =As.RegExp(@".*LeanFT.*"),
                Index = 1
            });

            leanFTLink.Click();
            browser.Close();
            Reporter.GenerateReport();
            SDK.Cleanup();

        }
    }
}
```

We can also write web tests using application model as
illustrated in below example. Please notice how we have
passed the browser to the calculator model.

```
using System;
using
Microsoft.VisualStudio.TestTools.UnitTesting;
using HP.LFT.SDK.Descriptions;
using HP.LFT.UnitTesting;
using HP.LFT.Common;
using HP.LFT.SDK.Web;
using HP.LFT.SDK;
using HP.LFT.Report;
using HP.LFT.SDK.StdWin;
using System.Diagnostics;

namespace leanFT
{
    [TestClass]
    public class UnitTest1
    {
        [TestMethod]
        public void TestCalculator()
        {
            SDK.Init(new SdkConfiguration());
            Reporter.Init(new
ReportConfiguration());

Process.Start(@"d:\Windows\System32\calc.exe");
            IWindow win =
Desktop.Describe<IWindow>(new WindowDescription
                {
                    IsOwnedWindow = false,
                    IsChildWindow = false,
                    WindowClassRegExp =
@"CalcFrame",
                    WindowTitleRegExp =
@"Calculator"
                });
```

```
        Trace.WriteLine("Calculator window
title is " + win.WindowTitleRegExp);
        var button8 =
win.Describe<HP.LFT.SDK.StdWin.IButton>(new
HP.LFT.SDK.StdWin.ButtonDescription
        {
            Text = string.Empty,
            WindowId = 138,
            NativeClass = @"Button"
        });
        button8.Click();

        var result =
win.Describe<IStatic>(new StaticDescription
        {
            WindowId = 150,
            NativeClass = @"Static"
        });
        Trace.WriteLine("Result text contains
" + result.Text);

        var calculatorModel = new
CalculatorModel();

calculatorModel.CalculatorWindow.ButtonPlus.Cli
ck();

calculatorModel.CalculatorWindow.Button3.Click(
);

calculatorModel.CalculatorWindow.ButtonEquals.C
lick();

        IBrowser browser =
BrowserFactory.Launch(BrowserType.InternetExplo
rer);
        var calculatorModel1 = new
CalculatorModel(browser);
```

```
calculatorModel1.GooglePage.SearchEditField.Set
Value("11");

        Trace.WriteLine("Result of addition
is " + result.Text);
        Assert.AreEqual("11", result.Text,
"Addition of 8 and 3");
        win.Close();
        Reporter.GenerateReport();
        SDK.Cleanup();


    }
  }
}
```

10.2 Identifying the elements using xpath and css

Below example illustrates how to use XPATH and CSS selectors to identify the web elements in LeanFT in C#.Net.

```
using System;
using
Microsoft.VisualStudio.TestTools.UnitTesting;
using HP.LFT.SDK;
using HP.LFT.Verifications;
using System.Diagnostics;
using System.Threading;
using HP.LFT.SDK.Web;

namespace LeanFtTestProject1
{
    [TestClass]
    public class LeanFtTest :
UnitTestClassBase<LeanFtTest>
    {
        [ClassInitialize]
```

```
        public static void
ClassInitialize(TestContext context)
        {
            GlobalSetup(context);
        }

        [TestInitialize]
        public void TestInitialize()
        {

        }

        [TestMethod]
        public void TestMethod1()
        {
            IBrowser browser =
BrowserFactory.Launch(BrowserType.Chrome);

            // Navigate to www.softpost.org

browser.Navigate("http://www.softpost.org/selen
ium-test-page/");

            // Find edit box using Xpath
            IEditField firstName =
browser.Describe <IEditField>(new
EditFieldDescription
            {
                XPath = "//input[@id='fn']"

            });

            firstName.SetValue("XPATH");

            // Find edit box using CSS
            firstName =
browser.Describe<IEditField>(new
EditFieldDescription
            {
                CSSSelector = "input[id='fn']"
```

```
            });

            firstName.SetValue("CSS");

            browser.Close();
        }

        [TestCleanup]
        public void TestCleanup()
        {
        }

        [ClassCleanup]
        public static void ClassCleanup()
        {
            GlobalTearDown();
        }
    }
}
```

10.3 Firing events

Below example illustrates how to fire the event on web objects in C#.Net. In below example, we have fired click event on the web link.

```
using System;
using
Microsoft.VisualStudio.TestTools.UnitTesting;
using HP.LFT.SDK.Web;

namespace LeanFtTestProject1
{
    [TestClass]
    public class FireEvents :
UnitTestClassBase<LeanFtTest>
```

```csharp
    {
        [ClassInitialize]
        public static void
ClassInitialize(TestContext context)
        {
            GlobalSetup(context);
        }

        [TestInitialize]
        public void TestInitialize()
        {

        }

        [TestMethod]
        public void FireEvent()
        {
            IBrowser browser =
BrowserFactory.Launch(BrowserType.InternetExplo
rer);
            // Navigate to www.softpost.org

browser.Navigate("http://www.softpost.org/selen
ium-test-page/");

            // Find Link Home
            ILink homeLink =
browser.Describe<ILink>(new LinkDescription
            {
                InnerText = "Home",
                Index = 0

            });

homeLink.FireEvent(EventInfoFactory.CreateMouse
EventInfo(MouseEventTypes.OnClick));

            browser.Sync();
```

```
            browser.Close();
        }

    [TestCleanup]
    public void TestCleanup()
    {
    }

    [ClassCleanup]
    public static void ClassCleanup()
    {
        GlobalTearDown();
    }
        }
    }
}
```

Note that we can fire various mouse events as shown in below image.

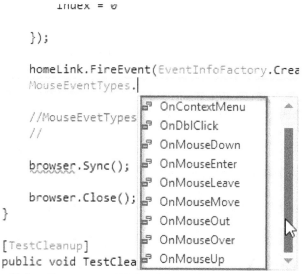

Firing Events on Web objects in LeanFT

10.4 Executing JavaScript

Below example illustrates how to execute java script in a web page in LeanFT. Note that RunJavaScript method of Page object to execute a JavaScript.

```
using System;
using
Microsoft.VisualStudio.TestTools.UnitTesting;
using HP.LFT.SDK.Web;

namespace LeanFtTestProject1
{
    [TestClass]
    public class JavaScriptTest :
UnitTestClassBase<LeanFtTest>
    {
        [ClassInitialize]
        public static void
ClassInitialize(TestContext context)
        {
            GlobalSetup(context);
        }

        [TestInitialize]
        public void TestInitialize()
        {

        }

        [TestMethod]
        public void ExecuteJavaScript()
        {
            IBrowser browser =
BrowserFactory.Launch(BrowserType.InternetExplo
rer);
            // Navigate to www.softpost.org
```

```
browser.Navigate("http://www.softpost.org/selen
ium-test-page/");
            browser.Sync();

            String html =
browser.Page.RunJavaScript("document.body.inner
HTML;");
            Console.WriteLine("HTML Source of
the page" + html);
            Console.WriteLine("Scrolling to
120,100");

browser.Page.RunJavaScript("window.scrollTo(120
,100);");

            String documentState =
browser.Page.RunJavaScript("document.readyState
");
            Console.WriteLine("Document State
is " + documentState);


            browser.Close();
        }

        [TestCleanup]
        public void TestCleanup()
        {
        }

        [ClassCleanup]
        public static void ClassCleanup()
        {
            GlobalTearDown();
        }
    }
}
```

11. Windows Application automation

11.1 Calculator automation using LeanFT

LeanFT supports testing of standard windows based applications, .Net applications, WPF applications etc.

Testing these applications is very easy with the help of Object Identification Center(OIC) tool which allows generating the code for the objects on the fly.

In sample test below, We are going to verify if calculator + operator is working correctly or not. If the result of 8+3 is 11, our test passes else it will fail.

Instead of using Description programming, we can also create the application model of the calculator using OIC. Application model in LeanFT is equivalent to the Object repository in UFT (QTP). In below example, we have used both approaches to test the calculator - Description as well as Application model.

```
using System;
using
Microsoft.VisualStudio.TestTools.UnitTesting;
using HP.LFT.SDK.Descriptions;
using HP.LFT.UnitTesting;
using HP.LFT.Common;
using HP.LFT.SDK.Web;
using HP.LFT.SDK;
using HP.LFT.Report;
using HP.LFT.SDK.StdWin;
using System.Diagnostics;

namespace leanFT
```

```
{
    [TestClass]
    public class UnitTest1
    {

        [TestMethod]
        public void TestCalculator()
        {
            SDK.Init(new SdkConfiguration());
            Reporter.Init(new
ReportConfiguration());

Process.Start(@"d:\Windows\System32\calc.exe");
            IWindow win =
Desktop.Describe<IWindow>(new WindowDescription
                {
                    IsOwnedWindow = false,
                    IsChildWindow = false,
                    WindowClassRegExp =
@"CalcFrame",
                    WindowTitleRegExp =
@"Calculator"
                });

            Trace.WriteLine("Calculator window
title is " + win.WindowTitleRegExp);


            var button8 =
win.Describe<HP.LFT.SDK.StdWin.IButton>(new
HP.LFT.SDK.StdWin.ButtonDescription
                {
                    Text = string.Empty,
                    WindowId = 138,
                    NativeClass = @"Button"
                });
            button8.Click();

            var result =
win.Describe<IStatic>(new StaticDescription
```

```
                {
                    WindowId = 150,
                    NativeClass = @"Static"
                });
            Trace.WriteLine("Result text contains
" + result.Text);

            var calculatorModel = new
CalculatorModel();

calculatorModel.CalculatorWindow.ButtonPlus.Cli
ck();

calculatorModel.CalculatorWindow.Button3.Click(
);

calculatorModel.CalculatorWindow.ButtonEquals.C
lick();
            Trace.WriteLine("Result of addition
is " + result.Text);
            Assert.AreEqual("11", result.Text,
"Addition of 8 and 3");
                win.Close();
                Reporter.GenerateReport();
                SDK.Cleanup();


            }
        }
}
```

11.2 Notepad Automation using LeanFT

Here is the example that illustrates how to automate
Notepad application.

```
using System;
using
Microsoft.VisualStudio.TestTools.UnitTesting;
using HP.LFT.SDK;
using HP.LFT.Verifications;
using System.Diagnostics;
using System.Threading;
using HP.LFT.SDK.StdWin;

namespace LeanFtTestProject1
{
    [TestClass]
    public class LeanFtTest :
UnitTestClassBase<LeanFtTest>
    {
        [ClassInitialize]
        public static void
ClassInitialize(TestContext context)
        {
            GlobalSetup(context);
        }

        [TestInitialize]
        public void TestInitialize()
        {

        }

        [TestMethod]
        public void TestMethod1()
        {
            Process appProcess = new Process {
StartInfo = { FileName =
@"C:\Windows\System32\notepad.exe" } };
            appProcess.Start();
```

```csharp
        Thread.Sleep(3000);

        IWindow notepadWindow =
Desktop.Describe<IWindow>(new WindowDescription
        {
            WindowClassRegExp = "Notepad",
            WindowTitleRegExp = " Notepad"
        });

        IEditor editor =
notepadWindow.Describe<IEditor>(new
EditorDescription
        {
            WindowClassRegExp = "Edit",
            NativeClass = "Edit"
        });

        editor.SendKeys("This is automated
text");

        Thread.Sleep(3000);
        notepadWindow.Close();

        IButton button =
Desktop.Describe<IWindow>(new WindowDescription
        {
            IsOwnedWindow = false,
            IsChildWindow = false,
            WindowClassRegExp = @"Notepad",
            WindowTitleRegExp = @" Notepad"
        }).Describe<IDialog>(new
DialogDescription
        {
            IsOwnedWindow = true,
            IsChildWindow = false,
            Text = @"Notepad",
            NativeClass = @"#32770"
        }).Describe<IButton>(new
ButtonDescription
```

```
        {
            Text = @"Do&n't Save",
            NativeClass = @"Button"
        });

        button.Click();
    }

    [TestCleanup]
    public void TestCleanup()
    {
    }

    [ClassCleanup]
    public static void ClassCleanup()
    {
        GlobalTearDown();
    }
    }
}
```

11.3 Automation of Java Applications

We can automate the Java applications developed in AWK and Swing. You need to ensure 2 things before you start the automation of Java based applications.

1. Load the Java add-in
2. Ensure that you use the using HP.LFT.SDK.Java namespace in your test

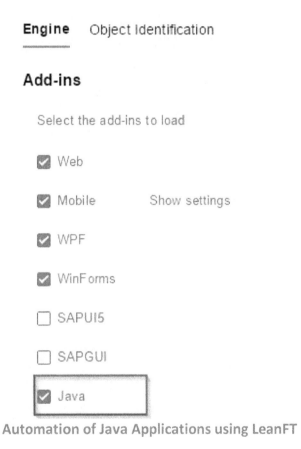

Automation of Java Applications using LeanFT

Here is the sample example that illustrates how to click on the checkbox in a Java app. Below code will start the Java App, then find the window with title - Bus App and then select the checkbox with attached text as C1.

```csharp
using
Microsoft.VisualStudio.TestTools.UnitTesting;
using HP.LFT.SDK;
using System.Diagnostics;
using HP.LFT.SDK.Java;

namespace LeanFtTestProject1
{
    [TestClass]
    public class JavaAppTest :
UnitTestClassBase<NotepadTest>
    {
        [ClassInitialize]
        public static void
ClassInitialize(TestContext context)
        {
            GlobalSetup(context);
        }

        [TestInitialize]
        public void TestInitialize()
        {

        }

        [TestMethod]
        public void TestMethod1()
        {
            // Launch Java Application
            var javaAppProcess = new Process {
StartInfo = { FileName = "java", Arguments = "-
jar myJavaApp.jar" } };
            javaAppProcess.Start();
```

```
        // Find main Java Window
        var window =
Desktop.Describe<IWindow>(new WindowDescription
        {
            Title = "Bus App",
            Index = 0
        });

        //Find the checkbox of in the Java
Window
        var checkBox =
window.Describe<ICheckBox>(new
CheckBoxDescription
        {
            AttachedText="C1"
        });

checkBox.SetState(CheckedState.Checked);

        }

        [TestCleanup]
        public void TestCleanup()
        {
        }

        [ClassCleanup]
        public static void ClassCleanup()
        {
            GlobalTearDown();
        }
    }
}
```

11.4 Automation of SAP Applications

We can automate the SAP applications using LeanFT with the help of SAP add-ins. You need to ensure 2 things before you start the automation of SAP applications.

1. Load the SAP add-ins
2. Ensure that you use the using HP.LFT.SDK.SAP namespace in your test

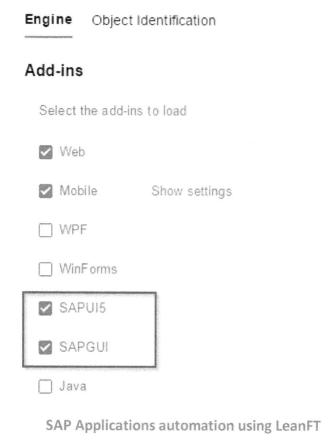

SAP Applications automation using LeanFT

Below example illustrates how to automate SAP app.

```
using
Microsoft.VisualStudio.TestTools.UnitTesting;
using HP.LFT.SDK;
using System.Diagnostics;
using HP.LFT.SDK.SAP.UI5;
using HP.LFT.SDK.Web;
using System.Threading;

namespace LeanFtTestProject1
{
    [TestClass]
    public class SAPTest :
UnitTestClassBase<NotepadTest>
    {
        [ClassInitialize]
        public static void
ClassInitialize(TestContext context)
        {
            GlobalSetup(context);
        }

        [TestInitialize]
        public void TestInitialize()
        {

        }

        [TestMethod]
        public void TestMethod1()
        {
            IBrowser browser =
BrowserFactory.Launch(BrowserType.InternetExplo
rer);

            // Open SAP application from test
page
```

```
browser.Navigate("https://sapui5.netweaver.onde
mand.com/sdk/#test-
resources/sap/ui/commons/ListBox.html");
            browser.Sync();
            Thread.Sleep(20000);

            // Find the Edit box.
            var editbox =
browser.Describe<HP.LFT.SDK.SAP.UI5.IEditField>
(new HP.LFT.SDK.SAP.UI5.EditFieldDescription
            {
                Id = @"txtFld"
            });

            // Enter the value in edit box
            editbox.SetValue("LeanFT");

        }

        [TestCleanup]
        public void TestCleanup()
        {
        }

        [ClassCleanup]
        public static void ClassCleanup()
        {
            GlobalTearDown();
        }
    }
}
```

11.5 Automation of .Net Applications

Below example illustrates how to automate .Net WinForms and WPF applications using LeanFT.

Note that for automating the WinForms applications, you will have to use below namespace.

```
using HP.LFT.SDK.WinForms;
```

Note that for automating the WPF applications, you will have to use below namespace.

```
using HP.LFT.SDK.WPF;
```

Also ensure that you have loaded the add-ins for WinForms and WPF.

Below example illustrates how to automate WPF application.

```
using
Microsoft.VisualStudio.TestTools.UnitTesting;
using HP.LFT.SDK;
using System.Diagnostics;
using HP.LFT.SDK.WPF;
using System.Threading;

namespace LeanFtTestProject1
{
    [TestClass]
    public class WinFormsAndWpf :
UnitTestClassBase<NotepadTest>
    {
        [ClassInitialize]
        public static void
ClassInitialize(TestContext context)
        {
```

```
            GlobalSetup(context);
        }

        [TestInitialize]
        public void TestInitialize()
        {


        }

        [TestMethod]
        public void TestMethod1()
        {
            Process appProcess = new Process
            {
                StartInfo = { FileName =
@"C:\Users\Sagar\Downloads\BusAppGUI.exe" }
            };
            appProcess.Start();

            // wait for app to open
            Thread.Sleep(3000);

            IWindow wpfWindow =
Desktop.Describe<IWindow>(new WindowDescription
            {
                WindowTitleRegExp = @"Bus
Application"
            });

            var custEditBox =
wpfWindow.Describe<IEditField>(new
EditFieldDescription
            {
                ObjectName = @"customerName"
            });

            // enter the name of customer
            custEditBox.SetText("Paul");
```

```
        }

        [TestCleanup]
        public void TestCleanup()
        {
        }

        [ClassCleanup]
        public static void ClassCleanup()
        {
            GlobalTearDown();
        }
    }
}
```

11.6 Using Visual Relational Identifier

Visual relational identifiers are used to identify the objects in relation with other objects on the screen.

Visual relational identifiers feature was added in UFT. LeanFT also supports it and helps us to identify objects relative to x and y axis.

We can create Visual relational identifiers (VRI) in 2 ways.

1. Description programming
2. Using application model

To understand the VRI feature in a better way, consider below image. Suppose developer has not given any unique property to the button 2. Also imagine that developer has only given unique properties to the button 1 and 5. We can easily find the button 2 object using VRI feature in this scenario.

We know that button 2 is located to the right of button 1 and below button 5. This information is enough to identify the button button 2.

```
var button2 = calculator.Describe<IButton>(
    new ButtonDescription
        {
        NativeClass = "Button",
        Vri =
            //button 1 is to the left of
button 2
                {
            new Relation
                    {
                TestObject = button1,
                HorizontalRelation =
HorizontalVriRelation.Left,
                },
            //button 5 is to above button 2
            new Relation
```

```
                {
            TestObject = button5,
            VerticalRelation =
VerticalVriRelation.Above,
                }
        }
    });
```

In similar way, we can add relations in Object identification center. Below image shows how we can add VRI properties to identify the test objects using application model editor (Similar to the Object repository manager in UFT/QTP)

12. Synchronization

We can add sync point in 2 ways.

1. WaitUntil method
2. Exists method

```
using System;
using
Microsoft.VisualStudio.TestTools.UnitTesting;
using HP.LFT.SDK;
using HP.LFT.Verifications;
using System.Diagnostics;
using System.Threading;
using HP.LFT.SDK.StdWin;

namespace LeanFtTestProject1
{
    [TestClass]
    public class SyncTest :
UnitTestClassBase<NotepadTest>
    {
        [ClassInitialize]
        public static void
ClassInitialize(TestContext context)
        {
            GlobalSetup(context);
        }

        [TestInitialize]
        public void TestInitialize()
        {

        }

        [TestMethod]
        public void TestMethod1()
        {
```

```
        Process appProcess = new Process {
            StartInfo = { FileName =
@"C:\Windows\System32\notepad.exe" } };
            appProcess.Start();

        IWindow notepadWindow =
Desktop.Describe<IWindow>(new WindowDescription
            {
                WindowClassRegExp = "Notepad",
                WindowTitleRegExp = " Notepad"
            });

            //wait until notepad is displayed
            bool isNotepadDisplayed =
notepadWindow.WaitUntil((notepad) => { return
notepad.IsVisible; });

            if (isNotepadDisplayed)
            {
                Console.WriteLine("Notepad
Window Exists");
            }
            else
            {
                Console.WriteLine("Notepad
Window does not Exist");
            }

            //Another way to add sync point in
LeanFT
            if (notepadWindow.Exists(2))
            {
                Console.WriteLine("Notepad
Window Exists");
            }
            else {
                Console.WriteLine("Notepad
Window does not Exist");
            }
```

```
        }

        [TestCleanup]
        public void TestCleanup()
        {
        }

        [ClassCleanup]
        public static void ClassCleanup()
        {
            GlobalTearDown();
        }
    }
}
```

13. Assertions and reports

13.1 Assertions in LeanFT

Assertions can be added in the LeanFT tests using Verify class as shown in below example. Note that Verify class has below methods.

1. AreEqual , AreNotEqual
2. IsTrue, IsFalse
3. StartsWith, Contains, EndsWith
4. LessOrEqual, Less, Greater, GreaterOrEqual
5. IsMatch
6. IsNullOrEmpty, IsNotNullOrEmpty

```
using System;
using
Microsoft.VisualStudio.TestTools.UnitTesting;
using HP.LFT.SDK;
using HP.LFT.Report;
using System.Diagnostics;
using System.Threading;
using HP.LFT.SDK.Web;
using System.Drawing;
using HP.LFT.Verifications;

namespace LeanFtTestProject1
{
    [TestClass]
    public class Assertions
    {
        [TestMethod]
        public void TestAssertions()
        {
            SDK.Init(new SdkConfiguration
            {
```

```
                ServerAddress = new
Uri("ws://localhost:5095")
            });

            ReportConfiguration r = new
ReportConfiguration();
            r.IsOverrideExisting = true;
            r.Title= "My LeanFT Report";
            Reporter.Init(r);

            IBrowser browser =
BrowserFactory.Launch(BrowserType.InternetExplo
rer);
            // Navigate to www.softpost.org

browser.Navigate("http://www.softpost.org/selen
ium-test-page/");

            // Find edit box using Xpath
            IEditField firstName =
browser.Describe<IEditField>(new
EditFieldDescription
            {
                XPath = "//input[@id='fn']"
            });

            firstName.SetValue("sagar");

            Verify.AreEqual("sagar",
firstName.Value,
                "Verifying the editbox value");

            browser.Close();

            Reporter.GenerateReport();
            SDK.Cleanup();
        }
    }
}
```

Below report shows that verification was successful.

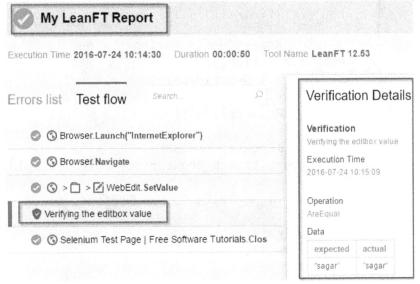

LeanFT report assertions and verifications

13.2 Generating reports with screenshots and recordings

We can customize the HTML report generated by LeanFT in various ways as shown in below example.

ReportConfiguration class allows you to configure the report name, target directory, report level etc. We can log custom messages in the report using Reporter.ReportEvent method. Note that ReportEvent method can also take a screenshot image as a parameter

```
using System;
using
Microsoft.VisualStudio.TestTools.UnitTesting;
using HP.LFT.SDK;
using HP.LFT.Report;
using System.Diagnostics;
using System.Threading;
using HP.LFT.SDK.Web;
using System.Drawing;

namespace LeanFtTestProject1
{
    [TestClass]
    public class Reports
    {
        [TestMethod]
        public void TestReports()
        {
            SDK.Init(new SdkConfiguration
            {
                ServerAddress = new
Uri("ws://localhost:5095")
            });

            ReportConfiguration r = new
ReportConfiguration();
            r.IsOverrideExisting = true;
            r.Title= "My LeanFT Report";
            Reporter.Init(r);

            IBrowser browser =
BrowserFactory.Launch(BrowserType.InternetExplo
rer);
            // Navigate to www.softpost.org

browser.Navigate("http://www.softpost.org/selen
ium-test-page/");

            // Find edit box using Xpath
```

```
        IEditField firstName =
browser.Describe<IEditField>(new
EditFieldDescription
        {
            XPath = "//input[@id='fn']"

        });

        firstName.SetValue("sagar");
        Image img = browser.GetSnapshot();
        Reporter.ReportEvent("Setting value
in edit box", "", Status.Passed, img);

        browser.Close();

        Reporter.GenerateReport();
        SDK.Cleanup();
    }
  }
}
```

Here is the HTML report generated by above code.

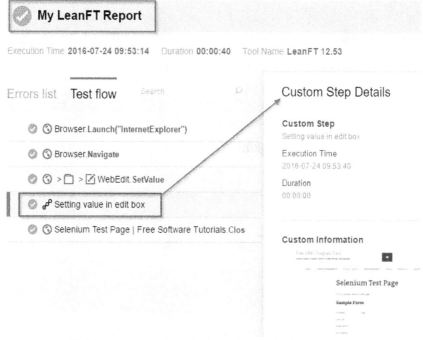

Taking screenshot in LeanFT in C#.Net

14. Converting UFT object repository into application model

LeanFT is backward compatible with your old repositories in QTP (UFT). You can easily convert old repositories into application models in C#.Net and Java.

LeanFT comes with a tool called as **OR2AppModelConverter** which can be used for converting the repositories into application models. You can find this tool in LeanFT installation folder in bin directory. It's a command line tool which you can invoke with below parameters.

OR2AppModelConverter ORFile AppModelFile

ORfile is the path to the repository file and AppModelFile (.tsrx file) is the path of the file which will be generated with application models.

Once Application model file is generated, you can easily use the test objects inside that repository as an application objects.

15. Frameworks in LeanFT

15.1 Keyword driven frameworks

Keyword driven frameworks are very popular in LeanFT.

Please follow below steps to create keyword driven framework.

1. Find main operations and features of the application.
2. Map each feature or operation to a keyword.
3. Write a code to automate specific keyword.
4. Create test sheet containing test cases made up of one or more keywords. You can store the test sheet in Excel file, Database or in the form of Unit test class.
5. Unless you are using Unit test class, you might need to create a driver script to execute each test case.

Here is the case study on WPF Flight application provided by HP.

In this application, we can create a keyword for each major feature like log in to the application, searching a flight, selecting a flight, Placing a order, Searching a order, Deleting the order, Cancelling the order, Book a flight, Verify flights.

Then we can create test cases for various user scenarios using same keywords as mentioned above.

Here are couple of test cases created using above keywords. Note that in below test cases, we have re-used login keyword.

Here is the test case to search for a flight.

1. Login to the Flight application.
2. Search for the flights from London to Paris in next week for one person.
3. Verify that flights are displayed from London to Paris only.

Here is the test case to search for a order.

1. Login to the Flight application.
2. Book a flight and note down order number say 88.
3. Search for order with id 88.
4. Verify that flight details are correctly displayed.

15.2 Data Driven Frameworks

Data driven framework are used when you need to test the application with various types of data.

You can store the data in below formats.

1. Microsoft Excel Files
2. Databases

In data driven frameworks, we test the same feature but with different set of data. For example, in HP flight application, we can test the Login functionality with various combination of User Id and Password.

Note that here Login functionality is same but Test data is different during each run.

15.3 SpecFlow

We can integrate the LeanFT tests with SpecFlow very easily. Please follow below steps.

1. Install SpecFlow extension for Visual Studio.
2. Add SpecFlow and SpecFlow Runner nuget packages in LeanFT project references.
3. Add feature files and step definitions.
4. Execute the scenarios.

Here is the sample feature file. In this feature file, there is a one scenario. We are checking that title of the notepad contains notepad word.

```
Feature: Notepad feature

@mytag
Scenario: Verify Notepad title
        Given NotePad is open
        Then I verify that title contains
"Notepad" word
```

Then here is the step definition file for above feature file. Note that we have added LeanFT code in the steps.

```
using HP.LFT.Report;
using HP.LFT.SDK;
using HP.LFT.SDK.StdWin;
using
Microsoft.VisualStudio.TestTools.UnitTesting;
using System;
using System.Diagnostics;
using TechTalk.SpecFlow;

namespace LeanFtTestProject1
{
    [Binding]
    public class NotepadFeatureSteps
    {
        IWindow notepadWindow;
        [Given(@"NotePad is open")]
        public void GivenNotePadIsOpen()
        {
            SDK.Init(new SdkConfiguration
            {
                ServerAddress = new
Uri("ws://localhost:5095")
            });
            ReportConfiguration r = new
ReportConfiguration();
            r.IsOverrideExisting = true;
            r.Title = "My LeanFT Report";

            Reporter.Init(r);

            Process appProcess = new Process
            {
                StartInfo = { FileName =
@"C:\Windows\System32\notepad.exe" }
            };
            appProcess.Start();
```

```
            notepadWindow =
Desktop.Describe<IWindow>(new WindowDescription
            {
                WindowClassRegExp = "Notepad",
                Index = 0
            });
        }


        [Then(@"I verify that title contains
""(.*)"" word")]
        public void
ThenIVerifyThatTitleContainsWord(string p0)
        {
            String title =
notepadWindow.WindowTitleRegExp;

Assert.IsTrue(title.ToLower().Contains(p0.ToLow
er()));
            notepadWindow.Close();
            SDK.Cleanup();
        }
    }
}
```

16. Integrating the LeanFT tests with CI servers

16.1 Adding MSBuild task in Bamboo

MSBuild is used to build .Net project.

MSBuild is used to build the .net project. It generates .dll file for the project. MSBuild task has 2 important settings.

1. executable - MSBuild executable
2. project file - .sln file of .net project

Below images show how to add MSBuild task in Bamboo.

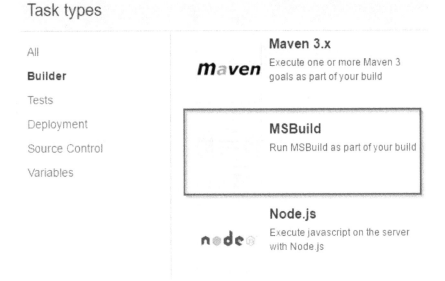

MSBuild task in Bamboo

Configure MSBuild in Bamboo

16.2 Adding MSTest task in Bamboo

MSTest is used to execute the tests from the container file in .Net project.

Below images show how to configure the MSTest in Bamboo.

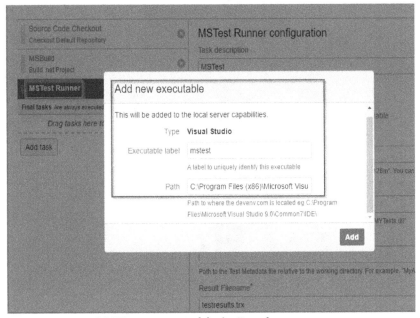

MSTest executable in Bamboo

MSTest configuration in Bamboo

Below image shows the sample MSTest log.

MSTest log in Bamboo

16.3 Jenkins

In this article, we will see how to create a build for Visual Studio .Net project in Jenkins.

You will need to install below plugins before you can create a .Net build in Jenkins.

1. MSBuild plugin for Jenkins
2. MSTest plugin for Jenkins

I have already explained how to install plugins in Jenkins in earlier posts. Once you have installed above plugins, you will have to change below settings in Jenkins System.

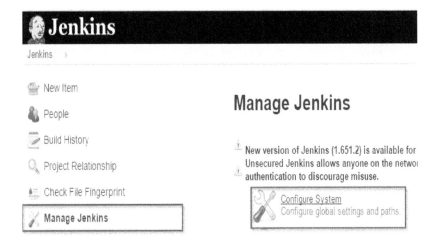

Configure Jenkins system

MSBuild

MSBuild installations

MSBuild

Name

MSBuild

Path to MSBuild   C:\Windows\Microsoft.NET\Framework64\v4.0.30319

Default parameters

MSBuild path configuration in Jenkins

MSTest

MSTest installations

MSTest

Name

MSTest

Path to MSTest   C:\Program Files (x86)\Microsoft Visual Studio 14.0\Common7\IDE

Default parameters

Omit NoIsolation

MSTest path configuration in Jenkins

Then you can create a new build project as explained in article on how to configure maven build in Jenkins.

SCM and Build trigger steps are similar for most of the projects. Now let us see how to add MSBuild and MSTest build tasks in .Net build.

Build

Build a Visual Studio project or solution using MSBuild

MSBuild Version

(Default)

MSBuild Build File

UnitTestProject1.sln

Command Line Arguments

MSBuild step in Jenkins

Run unit tests with MSTest

MsTest Version	(Default)
Test Files	UnitTestProject1\bin\Debug\UnitTestProject1.dll
Test Categories	
Result File Name	results

MSTest build step in Jenkins

Once .Net build configuration is saved, you can run the build from Jenkins Dashboard. Below image shows sample build log.

```
Done Building Project "C:\Program Files (x86)\Jenkins\jobs\Visual Studio Build\workspace\
(default targets).
Done Building Project "C:\Program Files (x86)\Jenkins\jobs\Visual Studio Build\workspace\

Build succeeded.
    0 Warning(s)
    0 Error(s)

Time Elapsed 00:00:03.62
Path To MSTest.exe: mstest.exe
Delete old result file file:/C:/Program%20Files%20(x86)/Jenkins/jobs/Visual%20Studio%20Bu
[workspace] $ mstest.exe /resultsfile:results "/testcontainer:C:\Program Files (x86)\Jenk
Build\workspace\UnitTestProject1\bin\Debug\UnitTestProject1.dll"
Microsoft (R) Test Execution Command Line Tool Version 14.0.23107.0
Copyright (c) Microsoft Corporation. All rights reserved.

Loading C:\Program Files (x86)\Jenkins\jobs\Visual Studio Build\workspace\UnitTestProject
Starting execution...

Results              Top Level Tests
-------              ---------------
Passed               UnitTestProject1.tests.UnitTest1.TestMethod1
1/1 test(s) Passed

Summary
-------
Test Run Completed.
  Passed  1
  ---------
  Total   1
Results file:  C:\Program Files (x86)\Jenkins\jobs\Visual Studio Build\workspace\results
Test Settings: Default Test Settings
Finished: SUCCESS
```

.Net build log in Jenkins

16.4 TeamCity

In this topic, we will learn how to add build steps for .Net project in TeamCity.

Some of the popular build steps for .Net project are given below.

1. .Net process runner
2. MSBuild
3. Visual Studio tests
4. Visual Studio project (.sln)

Below image shows how to configure MSBuild runner.

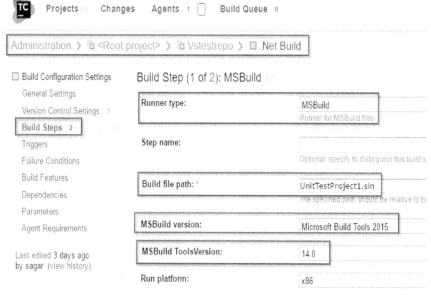

MSBuild runner in TeamCity

Below image shows how to configure Visual studio tests runner. There are 2 types of Test Engines available for running tests.

1. MSTest
2. VSTest

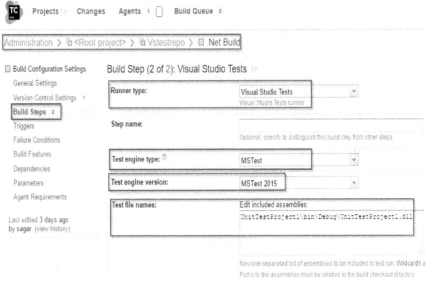

Visual Studio Tests runner in TeamCity

Below image shows the sample build log for above configuration.

.Net test build log in TeamCity

17. Challenges and solutions

17.1 Native objects

We can access native object properties and methods as shown in below example. Note that we have used NativeObject property to read the value in edit box.

```
IBrowser browser =
BrowserFactory.Launch(BrowserType.InternetExplo
rer);

// Navigate to www.softpost.org
browser.Navigate("http://www.softpost.org/selen
ium-test-page/");

// Find edit box using Xpath
 IEditField firstName =
browser.Describe<IEditField>(new
EditFieldDescription
            {
                XPath = "//input[@id='fn']"

            });

            firstName.SetValue("sagar");


Console.Out.WriteLine(firstName.NativeObject.va
lue);
            //string[] members = nativeElement;

            browser.Close();
```

17.2 LeanFT common issues and solutions

I have listed down common issues and solutions that you may encounter while working with LeanFT.

1. HP.LFT.Communication.SocketClient.Communicatio nException: Connect: Failed to connect to LeanFT runtime engine on....This exception comes when LeanFT runtime engine is not running. Just start the engine and this error should vanish.

2. HP.LFT.SDK.GeneralLeanFtException: An Internal problem has occurred, please make sure the LeanFT sdk was properly initialized....This exception comes when you have not initialized LeanFT sdk. To get rid of this exception, add below lines at the beginning of the code. SDK.Init(new SdkConfiguration());

3. Object not unique - This exception comes when LeanFT finds more than one object matching the description. To fix this issue, you need to add more properties so that only one object is identified.

4. Object not found - This exception comes when LeanFT is not able to find the object in the application. To fix this issue, ensure that object really exists in the application and you are using correct description to identify the object.

18. Comparison of LeanFT with Selenium and Ranorex

Based upon my experience, I can say that LeanFT and Ranorex are equivalent in terms of features.

Difference between Selenium and LeanFT

1. Biggest difference between Selenium and LeanFT (and Ranorex) is that Selenium can only support automation of web pages and not windows applications. But LeanFT and Ranorex can automate the windows and forms very easily along with web application.
2. Another major difference between Selenium and other 2 tools is that Selenium is free!

Difference between LeanFT and Ranorex

1. LeanFT is developed by HP while Ranorex is developed by Ranorex Gmbh.
2. Ranorex coding can be done only in C#.Net While LeanFT can be coded in C#.Net as well as Java.
3. Ranorex uses xpath to identify objects in windows as well as web applications. LeanFT uses property value pairs to identify the objects in Windows apps. LeanFT also supports xpath in web applications.

19. Difference between HP UFT and LeanFT.

Here is the list of differences between LeanFT and UFT (QTP).

1. UFT uses vbscript as a programming language. LeanFT uses .Net (C#, VB.Net) and Java as a programming language.
2. UFT uses description programming as well as object repository. LeanFT uses description programming and Application models.
3. We use object spy in UFT to view properties of the objects. In LeanFT, we use Object identification center to view properties of the object.
4. Cross browser testing is much easier and simpler in LeanFT.

20. LeanFT references and Resources for .Net

Here is the list of all references you might need to learn LeanFT.

1. http://leanft-help.saas.hpe.com/en/12.52/HelpCenter/Content/HelpCenterRoot/DemoApps.htm – Demo applications provided by HP
2. http://leanft-help.saas.hpe.com/en/12.52/NetSDKReference/webframe.html – LeanFT .Net API
3. http://leanft-help.saas.hpe.com/en/12.52/HelpCenter/Content/HowTo/UFT_OR_Converter.htm – Coverting UFT Object repository into Application models in LeanFT
4. http://leanft-help.saas.hpe.com/en/12.52/HelpCenter/Content/HowTo/RunRemotely.htm – Executing the tests remotely in LeanFT
5. http://leanft-help.saas.hpe.com/en/12.52/HelpCenter/Content/HowTo/CI_Tools.htm – Integrating LeanFT with CI servers like TeamCity

www.ingramcontent.com/pod-product-compliance
Lightning Source LLC
Chambersburg PA
CBHW060949050326
40689CB00012B/2615